Praise for

The December Dozen

"If you have ever been curious about the many holidays that occur in December, or the origins of why we celebrate the way we do, you will love this book. Filled with twelve holidays, their origins, and a succinct explanation of why and how they are celebrated, you can learn easy ways to incorporate new traditions into your own celebrations to make your holidays even more merry and bright."

—*Valerie Costa, Special Features Editor, The Union*

"*The December Dozen: A Celebration of Holidays* is at the top of this Santa's list as the perfect book for the season!*"*

—*Loren Smith, San Diego's Surfing Santa*
and reality TV star of Santas in the Barn

"Cristina Smith masterfully blends the festive with the meaningful, the modern with the ancient, and the mystical with the magical in this fun yet sacred guide to honoring the season both out in the world and in our own inner sanctums."

—*Ingrid Coffin, founding minister of the*
Blue Sky Ranch Fellowship community

"This book is all about being open to new ideas and jumping into new experiences, which is the essence of being interculturally creative. The first step to connecting and belonging is becoming aware of the beauty of our commonalities while celebrating our many differences. Bring diversity and inclusion into your family's December with this meaningful and fun book! *The December Dozen* is a welcome invitation to explore, honor, and respect many cultures while celebrating the season. I highly recommend it."

–Genein M. Letford, M.Ed, Intercultural Creativity® founder, author, speaker

"Cristina Smith's newest book *The December Dozen* is a fascinating reminder to its readers that the winter holiday season is so much more than a time to simply spend money, visit malls, and eat large quantities of special holiday food. It is rather a time of year that is richly steeped with history, crossing multiple cultures and beliefs, and imbued with the traditions of many cultures. She reminds us that the Christmas season – by any of its many names – is a sensory experience of ceremonies and celebrations that bring people together throughout the world through their own customs. More than a merely a historical perspective, *The December Dozen* invites us along as armchair travelers as we savor the delights of this holiday season around the world. I especially love the larger idea that in our celebrations we are locking arms and hearts with many around the planet, that we truly live in a vibrant global community. I will probably never take Christmas for granted again. Thank you, Cristina! I'm off to plan my Saturnalia party!"

–Karen Stuth, author, A Speckled Stone: Thirty-one Poems for Seekers; The Wisdom of Tula Card Deck; *co-creator,* Quintangled: A Game of Strategy, Chance & Destiny, *and contributing author to* Life Wisdom Word Search: Yoga for the Brain

"Everything Cristina writes about in her books is about our choice of what to do with the great gift of life we have been given. She has experienced in her own life the power of the spirit to transform which allows her to tap into her energy and enthusiasm to help others become all they can be. Cristina helps us to learn to live fully in this present moment. Highly recommended!"

–*Dr. Russell Fanelli, Professor Emeritus,*
Western New England University

"Set your board games aside as *The December Dozen* is the perfect way to reconnect with friends and family this holiday season. You'll be inspired to do a fun activity, prepare a new dish or even host a night of trivia. Don't visit your friends and family this holiday without packing this little gem in your bag."

–*Suzette Webb, author of* Blues to Blessings:
Moving from Fearful to Faithful

"Cristina Smith thinks deeply and writes with the kind of simplicity and clarity that only comes from an almost cellular attunement to her subjects. Without pretense or posturing, she uplifts me."

–*Steven Forrest, bestselling author of* The Inner Sky

"Cristina Smith with Melissa Morgan have created a fabulous educational, informative, and supportive book for all readers! This was such a fun read. It creates great opportunity for teaching children about the diversity and foundations of our holiday season, like nothing I have seen before. It brings to life our northern hemisphere holiday traditions. What fun! I highly recommend it!"

–*Darity Wesley, author,* How To Be The REAL You!

"I love this gem of a book. It has beautiful photos and wonderful, endearing descriptions of *The December Dozen* holiday celebrations. Perfect to read as you snuggle up with a warm beverage. I learned so much about other cultures in this delightful book. It gave me a new appreciation for our diversity and the miracles of our similarities where love and light are celebrated around the world. This beauty by Cristina and Melissa will enhance your Decembers for years to come."

–*Janette Stuart, Angelic Practitioner and author of*
On a Path to Joy, Volumes One-Four

"Cristina Smith's fun and easily accessible works brilliantly blend quantum consciousness-based science with profound philosophical wisdom."

–*Amit Goswami, PhD, Quantum physicist and bestselling author of* The Self-Aware Universe

"As the world becomes more aware of different cultures, Smith has gifted us all with ideas and insights about the variety of traditions we can celebrate with our friends and neighbors. Her attention to detail and inclusivity is inspiring!"

–*Camille Leon, founder, Holistic Chamber of Commerce*

The
December
Dozen

A Celebration
of Holidays

The
December
Dozen

Cristina Smith
with Melissa Morgan

A YOGA FOR THE BRAIN BOOK

ISBN: 979-8-9851276-0-7 (paperback)
ISBN: 979-8-9851276-1-4 (ebook)

The December Dozen: A Celebration of Holidays
©2021 by Cristina Smith
All Rights Reserved

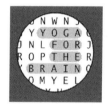

Nevada City, California
YogaForTheBrain.com

Published in the United States of America

Download your free companion
Yoga for the Brain word search puzzle
for this book at:
www.DecemberDozen.com

Table of Contents

Introduction

Welcome to the stories, history, and magic of what many people call the most wonderful time of the year! December is a month rich in opportunities to gather, celebrate, observe traditions, and share our light. We are excited to share with you these dozen delightful holidays. Some you've been familiar with your whole life and others may be totally new. In the spirit of supporting a global community of inclusion and unity through diversity, dive right in to some fascinating stories of faith, hope, love, and miracles.

Much of the northern hemisphere is encouraged to start to think about the holidays in mid-October, when retailers begin promoting December merchandise. By the time we get near Halloween, we know that in the United States, Thanksgiving is just around the corner. Next comes the whirlwind that takes us straight through to the New Year. There are so many possible holidays and rich traditions to enjoy. Hanukkah, Saturnalia, Winter Solstice, Yule, Christmas, Kwanzaa: it's a downright cornucopia of delight. We can celebrate our common humanity through our December diversity.

It's a time of contrasts. We turn inward and reflective. We reach out to each other to share our love and traditions. Rich historical precedent for these winter holidays reminds us that celebrating the turning of the seasons and the changing of the light is a human thing.

What's your temperature on the whole December experience? Does it seem like gladness or madness to you? Or somewhere in between? Do you dread December's arrival or look forward to it with glee? Do you have a to-do list that makes Santa's look like a text? Are you excited and energized? Or do you want to jump back into bed and pull the covers over your head?

With weather, logistics, shopping, and party planning, this time of year can stress out even the calmest soul. If we have recently lost a loved one, it could be a deep dive into grief or a powerful time of celebratory remembrance.

Meanwhile, we're heading into the shortest day of the year. How can that happen when we have so much to *do*? Ah, but remember, the shortest day translates into the longest night. How are you going use it?

This year, consider widening your focus. Add some variety to your observances, activities, and ideas. Spice up your holiday celebrations with worldwide traditions that are inclusive, comprehensive, fun, meaningful, and inspiring.

Bake or taste a Yule log or some gingerbread. Eat a tamale or some dumplings as something completely different to intrigue the holiday palate. Enjoy a simple meal of rice. Light candles to celebrate miracles in all forms. Keep yourself flexible on all levels. Our minds are so busy with happenings and obligations. Take time to have fun and remember to check in with your inner self. See if you can find some overarching themes that exist throughout time and across cultures. Light, trees, candles, miracles, greenery, hope, rising joy.

Whatever is going on in your outer world at this time, see if you can discover some joy. Lightness and diversity can always help. Celebrations can take any and many forms. A quiet and alone shower or bath can be a sacred act and a reminder that you're important too. We all matter. There are so many ways to honor ourselves and each other.

Winter is coming. It is often a more inward-focused time; at least Mother Nature tells us so. Even in the midst of holiday joy, quiet time, with ourselves can reap huge rewards. And it's often in these moments that we come up with the perfect party idea or think of just the right gift for the person on our list who has always been hard to buy or create for!

In this book, we share stories about twelve different ancient and modern December traditions, including suggestions for you and your family on how to welcome and honor them. The authors have celebrated some of these December days for decades and others they started incorporating more recently. There is no attempt to culturally appropriate any of these sacred days.

We are here to encourage inclusion, joy, education, and diversity which are some of the benefits of our connected, multicultural society. If you want to discover more in-depth information about any of the December dozen, seek someone out who is a longtime celebrant. They will have enriching insights and traditions to inspire. We all end up learning more about ourselves and each other.

However and whenever you participate in December holiday gladness, add some joy, delight, and play into the mix.

Enjoy a quiet sacred moment. Light a candle in honor of the return of the light. Remember to stoke your own inner flame. And have some fun!

Winter Solstice

Which holiday has the most ancient roots? It doesn't really matter, though the winter solstice is certainly in the running. The latest research on Stonehenge and earlier implies that winter solstice celebrations go back to prehistoric times. How cool would it be to add something to your holidays that went back to ancestors when they were in the times of hunter/gatherers? Talk about time-transcending resonance!

In the northern hemisphere, it was imperative for our ancestors to know the light cycles. They marked the lengthening days, the return of the light, the Sun. It was essential for survival. The light determined when to plant, harvest their crops, and hunt for food.

Marking the winter solstice was key to managing food stores and preparing for the future. Putting aside enough for winter and making sure seed was available for spring planting was life and death critical. As the eons passed, the advent of the Son was incorporated, integrated, and layered onto this natural earth cycle of the turning of the seasons.

We may not face the same decisions that our ancestors did, yet storage and supply remain important for us all. Bringing awareness, preparedness, and personal choice into things like our grocery supplies impacts everyone. Many of us have had to re-evaluate just what our needs are, from work to health to education to shelter. Pondering our options is traditional for this time of year.

The winter solstice, the shortest day of the year, occurs on December 21st or 22nd, depending on the year. This longest night is a peak of natural energy. Amidst the craziness of outward doingness, the energies have been sending us within, inviting us to simply *be* in silence and deep inner exploration. This quiet *be* time is as important as the busy *do* time in keeping us balanced and at peace with ourselves. Consider humming a tune of *do be do be do* to check in with yourself and make sure you aren't going off the deep end of too much to *do do* to the detriment of your deepest self. Consider this your sanity clause to partner with the season's jolly old elf, Santa Claus himself.

This internal process begins in late September with the autumnal equinox, when day and night are equal. This inward journey is available to assist deeply personal transformational processes. Picture the shifting of the season like the removing of a candle from the inside of an altar. The altar is your inner landscape and it is now time for the light within to break forth into the world. Like the return of longer days, this process does not have to happen all at once. It can grow organically, day-by-day, step-by-step.

Cultures globally celebrate this time of the year as the return of the light, when the duration of daylight begins to increase until reaching the spring equinox, when day and night are of equal length again.

No one is really sure when humans recognized the winter solstice and began heralding it as a turning point. An utterly astonishing array of ancient cultures worldwide built their greatest architectures so that they aligned with the solstices and equinoxes. Tombs, temples, cairns, and sacred observatories were oriented to take advantage of solstice light. Even cultures that followed a moon-based calendar incorporate the importance of these sun-based turning points.

One of our earliest civilizations, the Mesopotamians in the modern-day Middle East, had the first recorded winter solstice celebration. *Zagmuk* was a twelve-day festival of renewal, designed to commemorate the triumph of Marduk, patron deity of Babylon. Marduk was famous for fighting and taming the monsters of chaos during the longest night. His people believed that his triumph brought another year of safety and plenty.

Four thousand years ago, give or take a couple of centuries, ancient Egyptians marked the rebirth of the sun at this time of year. The festival lasted twelve days to reflect the twelve divisions in their solar calendar. They decorated with greenery, an ancient example that has led us to the Christmas tree and the evergreen holiday tradition. The

Egyptians used palms with twelve shoots as a symbol of the completed year.

Winter solstice is also a part of the cultural heritage of Pakistan and Tibet. In China, even though the calendar is based on the moon, the day of the solstice is observed.

Easy Ways to Celebrate

★ Take advantage of the long nights. Do some star gazing or commune with the moon.

★ Do an art project celebrating the sun.

★ Savor a beautiful sunrise.

★ Pick an herb from your garden, or view your trip to the grocery store as a hunter/gatherer experience.

★ Organize some of your chaos.

★ Greet the sun when you get up in the morning.

★ Decide to be bright and sunny on a day that you feel less than perfect.

★ Meditate on your innermost being and connection to the Divine.

★ Do something to offer your light to the world.

★ Shine on!

Dongzhi

How do they celebrate the winter solstice on the other side of the world? In a remarkably similar fashion, with food, family, and good times.

Winter solstice observances in China have been recorded for 2500 years. The ancient Chinese marked the turning point by observing the length of shadows. Since 202 BCE, the winter solstice has been known as *Dongzhi Festival. Dong* means *winter* and *zhi* means *arrival*. Pronounced *dong-zee* in American English, this important festival is the equivalent of Thanksgiving in the United States, and is usually observed between December 21st and 23rd, depending on the year.

Having its origins in the concept of *yin* and *yang* in Chinese philosophy, Dongzhi represents balance and harmony in life. The yin qualities of darkness and cold reach their height of influence on the shortest day of the year. They also mark a turning point for the coming of the light and warmth of yang.

Over the centuries, people began to honor their ancestors and gods on Dongzhi. Beginning in the Ming Dynasty (1368-1644) until 1911, observances grew ever grander, and the emperor would worship Heaven on this day. People would visit relatives and friends, give gifts, write poems, worship and pray to the gods and ancestors and pay respect to the elders.

Since 1912, the winter solstice has not been observed in as grand a fashion as in the ancient times. However, some folk customs have been passed down, especially around food.

There is an old story about the dumplings served during Dongzhi. As the legend goes, there was a renowned medical scientist at the end of the Eastern Han Dynasty (25-220 CE) by the name of Zhang Zhongjing. He'd been away from his village for some time and when he came home, he found the people suffering from hunger and cold. Some even had terrible blisters in their ears. To help them, Zhang Zhongjing cooked ear-shaped dumplings, stuffed with medicine and other ingredients that were warming. The villagers soon recovered, which led to the legend that not having dumplings on the winter solstice would lead to frozen ears.

Traditional dishes vary with the region. The north emphasizes foods considered warming in traditional Chinese medicine. The warming qualities help ensure a healthy respiratory system. Presently, the most popular customs are that dumplings are eaten in north China and *tang yuan,* brightly colored rice flour balls, in the south.

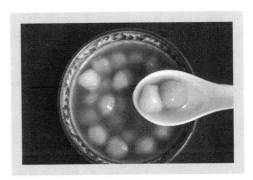

Another much loved food is *tsampa,* a dish that is considered integral to Tibetan culture. It is a hearty, nutty-tasting flour made from roasted barley and mixed by hand with butter tea, dried *dri* cheese (the dri is the female of the yak species), and sometimes sugar, to form a dough.

Easy Ways to Celebrate

- ★ Snuggle up and be cozy.

- ★ Eat or drink something warming for a holiday glow.

- ★ Honor your ancestors and pay respect to your elders.

- ★ Make a batch of dumplings or enjoy them out with your whole family.

- ★ Ask your grandparents for a story from their lives, or tell one if the folks are not available.

- ★ Make some food to share with an elder.

- ★ Treat your food as medicine.

Soyal

In one of many Native American traditions, the Hopi *Soyal* ceremony culminates on the shortest day of the year. Meaning *Establishing Life Anew for All the World*, Soyal helps create a plan of life for the coming year. The sun is turned back toward its summer path through prayers and rituals.

The Hopi people have lived in northern Arizona for over a thousand years. In their tradition, December is when the kachinas come down from their home in the San Francisco mountain peaks to bring the sun back to the world. The *katsinam* or *kachinas* are spirits that guard over the Hopi and dance at the winter solstice. There are more than 250 different types of katsinam who represent various beings, from animals to clouds. They are seen as spirit messengers who bring gifts of prosperity and life teachings to humankind.

Soyal can last up to sixteen days. Sacred rituals are performed in underground chambers called *kivas*. On the west

wall of the kiva, an altar is constructed with two or more ears of corn contributed from each family, surrounded by husks and stalks.

Some ceremonies involve dance and song. The kachinas may bring gifts to the children. This is the time of year when

elders pass down their stories. Important lessons are taught, including respect for others and a peaceful approach to life.

In preparation for the kachinas' arrival, the Hopi make prayer sticks of feathers and pinyon needles to bless the community. Homes, animals, and plants are all blessed. Children are given replicas of the kachinas, intricately carved and dressed like the dancers.

Though the sacred rituals are private, the Soyal traditionally ends with a public kachina dance. The katsinam are believed to remain with the Hopi people for six months, until the summer solstice, the longest day of the year. The kachinas then return to the mountains.

Easy Ways to Celebrate

★ Create your own prayer arrows from sticks and yarn.

★ Sing and dance.

★ Teach peace.

★ Plan for the coming year.

★ Listen to a story or tell one.

★ Bless and celebrate your corn before you eat it, or as you add it to a recipe.

★ Ponder the role of helpers in your daily life.

★ Give a child a doll or representative toy.

★ Bless your home and everyone in it.

Yalda

Yet another winter solstice celebration is *Yalda*, observed by Iranians around the world. Persia became Iran in 1935. Yalda is one of the most ancient Persian festivals, and dates back to the time when a majority of Persians were followers of Zoroastrianism, prior to the advent of Islam. Yalda, which means *birth*, is also known as *Shab-e Chelleh*. Coinciding with the beginning of winter, Yalda is an occasion to celebrate the end of the crop season. Today, it is a time when people are thankful for all blessings and pray for prosperity in the new year.

Yalda celebrates the arrival of winter, the renewal of the sun, and the victory of light over darkness. Yalda eve, which occurs on the winter solstice, is the night commemorating the birth of Mithra.

Mithra was the Persian god of the rising sun, contracts, covenants, and friendships. He also oversaw the orderly change of the seasons and maintained cosmic order. Additionally, he bestowed divine grace on kings which legitimized their rule. Mithra had his roots in India and remained a potent symbol of worship as the sun god throughout the subsequent centuries into the Roman Empire. He served as a protector of the faithful.

On Yalda night, family members gather, often in the house of the eldest member. As days start lengthening, ancient Persians believe that at the end of the first night of winter, darkness is defeated by light. Therefore, they must celebrate from dark until dawn.

Foods usually include fresh fruits and colorful *ajil*, which is a mixture of dried fruits, seeds, and nuts. Ajil is served in floral bowls. Tradition states that those who begin winter by eating summer fruits will not fall ill during the cold season; that's why eating watermelon is one of the most important customs on this night. Pomegranates, placed on top of a fruit basket, are reminders of the cycle of life, the rebirth and revival of generations. The color of the outer covering of a pomegranate symbolizes birth or dawn, and their bright red seeds, the glow of life.

Following a hot dinner, celebrants recite poetry, narrate stories, chant, play musical instruments, or just chat cozily. One of the other traditions of Yalda night is the reading of the classic poetry of Hafez, the fourteenth century Persian poet. Each member of the family makes a wish and randomly opens the book and asks the eldest to read it aloud. What is expressed in that poem is believed to be the interpretation of the wish and whether and how it will come true. This is called *Faal-e Hafez* (Hafez Omen).

EASY WAYS TO CELEBRATE

★ Count your blessings, saying them aloud and/or writing them down.

★ Do a poem divination or just read one of your favorites aloud to others.

★ Create an *ajil.*

★ Eat summer fruit, especially watermelon.

★ Place a pomegranate in your home.

Bodhi Day

Welcome to the Om Zone!

Bodhi Day is the Buddhist celebration of the Buddha's awakening or enlightenment. It is observed on December 8th as *Rōhatsu* (pronounced row-ah-sue) in Japan, and varying dates of the 8th day of the 12th lunar month based on the Chinese calendar in other countries. Why not observe both?

It is typical for Zen monks and laypeople to stay up the entire night before Rōhatsu meditating. The holiday is often preceded by an intensive time of fasting and internal self-examination.

Here's the story. We've all heard the legend of how Buddha

gained enlightenment sitting and meditating under a Bodhi tree. Turns out a Bodhi tree is a fig tree, now known as the sacred fig. *Bodhi* is another word for enlightenment.

There was an historical Buddha. He was a young Indian prince named Siddharta who lived more than 2,500 years ago. There are many legends about how Buddha's enlightenment came about.

The bottom line is that Siddharta had to overcome what we all do when we start to meditate. Distractions, self-doubt, and the mind's restless murmuring. Emotions, from anger to rage to grief to joy, all become distractions. Past and future entice the mind to dance elsewhere rather than deepening focus. His mental state was eventually described as like a still, clear pool.

Siddhartha finally found the answers he sought and became Enlightened. As a result, he experienced *Nirvana*, a state of transcendental bliss. Having done so, Siddhartha then became a Buddha or *Awakened One*. Up from that pool bubbled up all of the wisdom we associate with Buddhism today in its various forms.

For Buddhists all over the world, Bodhi Day is a time to remember Siddhartha and to meditate. It is traditional to eat one meal of rice and milk. This was the food offered to the Buddha by a girl named Sujata after his awakening. Candles and lights are lit on this day and kept burning, or turned on, for the next thirty days to symbolize enlightenment.

Like many December traditions, homes may have a small tree to decorate, often a ficus, which is a type of fig. Colored lights and beads connected with a string are used to symbolize that all things are united. A veritable rainbow of decorations adorn houses and little statues of the Buddha are scattered about, signifying that there are many ways to attain enlightenment.

Though you may not have a Buddhist bone in your body and it's not your cup of spiritual tea, consider taking some time to sit quietly and meditate on all you are grateful for. Review some of what you've realized over the course of this year, maybe even jotting them down in a journal. Put an ornament on your holiday tree or altar to acknowledge yourself. Savor a wonderful beverage and allow your mind to empty.

Say a little prayer for yourself, your loved ones, and all of your fellow Earthlings.

Be at peace with yourself and your life. Right here. Right now.

Easy Ways To Celebrate

★ Enjoy a simple meal of rice and milk.

★ Meditate.

★ Sit under or hug a tree.

★ Practice mindfulness.

★ Contemplate your navel.

★ Add colorful decorations to your home.

★ Take a moment and simply breathe. Ahhhh...

Mindfulness and Gratitude

This is a great time of year to count our blessings and teach respect and kindness for ourselves and others.

It's also a great time to be grateful. Gratitude is a funny thing. Sometimes it feels awkward, especially when times are hard. Like any habit, it takes cultivation.

Even if it does feel awkward, gratitude is an amazing stress reliever. Experiment with telling yourself three things every day that you're grateful for. We can all be grateful for obvious things that we tend to take for granted. Many of us still have access to hot and cold running water, lights, electricity, heat, and avenues to abundant food. This makes us immeasurably blessed and more fortunate than a large percentage of the world's population.

We can be especially grateful for those we love who love us back. Let those loved ones know how important they are. Hug your friends, family, and loved ones. Hugs don't have to be physical to be felt and enjoyed. Send a card or a thoughtful text. Schedule an old-fashioned phone call or modern video call and have a chat. Send pictures. Spread the love.

Include animal companions in your holiday celebrations. The Buddha was known for his compassion for animals. Think of all the love and joy they bring. Aren't we lucky to share their lives? Recognize the love and lessons that they are so very good at sharing with us.

Take a moment for nature. Feel the planet beneath your feet. Thank it for its many services, from growing nourishing food to giving us a place to stand and shelter. Acknowledge the trees and the wind and the wild animals. The bees. So many pieces to our Earth puzzle. Let's harmonize as much as we can.

Feel the light of the moon and stars upon your face as the time of darkness lingers and grows. And celebrate the return of the sun, and/or the Son. Light within and without matters. Stoke your inner flames and shine your beautiful unique light.

This world needs all of us.

St. Nicholas Day

Who doesn't love Santa Claus? It would take a Scrooge indeed! Jolly old St. Nicholas. He actually was an historical person. Who knew?

St. Nicholas was an early Christian bishop in the fourth century, during the time of the Roman Empire. He was bishop of Myra, which is now called Demre, in modern day Turkey. He became the patron saint of Russia and Greece as well as a number of cities. Saint Nicholas Day is celebrated on December 6th.

St. Nicholas was noted for his generosity, and gave away all of his inherited wealth. He traveled the countryside helping the poor and sick. He became known as the protector of children and sailors. One of the legends of his good works was how he saved three impoverished girls by paying their marriage dowries in gold.

In the 1600s, because of the Reformation, St. Nicholas was largely forgotten in Protestant Europe, although his memory was kept alive in Holland as *Sinter Klaas*. St. Nicholas arrived on horseback on his feast day, dressed in a bishop's red robe and miter (the pointy hat), accompanied by Black Peter (Zwarte Piet), variously described as a freed slave or a Moor. Together they distributed sweets and presents to good children or lumps of coal, potatoes, or switches to bad ones.

St. Nicholas first entered American popular culture in the late eighteenth century in New Amsterdam (New York), when Dutch families gathered to honor the anniversary of the death of *Sint Nikolaas* (Dutch for Saint Nicholas), or *Sinter Klaas* for short. *Santa Claus* draws his name from this abbreviation. Welcome Santa! We're so glad you made it down the chimney! Whether we have one or not!

St. Nicholas' legend of a kindly and generous old man was united with Nordic folktales of a magician who rewarded good children and punished naughty ones. The resulting image of Santa Claus in the United States crystallized in the nineteenth century. He has ever since remained the patron of the gift-giving festival of Christmas. In Britain he is largely known as Father Christmas.

In parts of northern Europe, St. Nicholas Day has remained a time when children are given special cookies, candies, and gifts. In many places, children leave letters for St. Nicholas and carrots or grass for his donkey or horse. In the morning, they find goodies under their pillows or in the shoes, stockings, or plates they have set out for him. Oranges and chocolate coins are common treats. The coins remind us of St. Nicholas' legendary generosity. Good old St. Nick is responsible for candy canes too, due to their shape like a shepherd's crook or bishop's crosier. Peppermint! Yum!

Easy Ways To Celebrate

* ★ Give someone money unexpectedly.

* ★ Eat an orange.

* ★ Make food for someone who is ill.

* ★ Leave a candy cane out to remind you of the generosity and spirit of St. Nicholas. Or eat a candy cane or share one!

* ★ Look at a picture of Santa Claus and his reindeer with newly inspired eyes.

* ★ Be generous with a child.

Las Posadas

What could be more fun than a party where you visit different neighbors' homes, sing songs, act out a play, enjoy great food, have toys and surprises, and enjoy your community, family, and friends? And honor your beliefs at the same time? *Las Posadas* is exactly that.

The community festivities of Las Posadas are a wonderful part of holiday celebrations in Mexico. They are rapidly spreading north into the United States. Las Posadas take place from December 16th to the 24th, the nine nights leading up to Christmas.

In Spanish, the word *posada* means *inn* or *shelter*. The biblical story of Mary and Joseph's search for an inn and journey to Bethlehem is acted out. There is a special song, Christmas carols, and a delightful party.

The tradition started in Mexico City as a series of extra masses in the 1500s. It seems to be one of many examples of how the Catholic religious traditions in Mexico were adapted to make it easier for the indigenous people to understand

them and blend them with their earlier beliefs. The Aztecs had a tradition of honoring their god Huitzilopochtli at the same time of year, coinciding with the winter solstice.

Early Posada celebrations were first held in churches. As the custom spread, celebrations were moved to the multi-family haciendas, and then to family homes. Starting in the nineteenth century, Las Posadas gradually evolved into the neighborhood celebrations of today.

It all gets started with a candlelit procession. (There're those candles again! One of the themes we see throughout cultures.) Those chosen to play Mary and Joseph lead the way, symbolically or in person. Everyone sings Christmas carols as they head to neighbors' houses. Different families host each night. Part of the heart of the celebration, *La Canción Para Pedir Posada,* a special song, is sung.

The song comes in two parts. Joseph's part is sung by those outside, asking for a place to stay. Those inside the house sing back, claiming there's no room. Back and forth they go until those inside relent and the door is opened. The party begins!

A short religious service gets things started, with readings from the Bible and prayer. Once the party gets going, it can be anything the hosts imagine. Elegant and fancy or down home just us folks and all points in between.

Las Posadas, like Kwanzaa, encourages contemplation of various principles for the different nights. They are: *humility, strength, detachment, charity, trust, justice, purity, joy,* and *generosity.* After the Bible reading and prayer, it's time to break out the food and warm drink.

Tamales are served, along with *ponche,* a traditional Mexican fruit punch with some of the main ingredients being fruit juice, guava, and hawthorn which is a hot corn-based drink. Atole is sometimes flavored with chocolate, pineapple, or other fruit.

Piñatas come next, with lots of fun and excitement for all. Piñatas are colorful hollow creations usually made of papier-mâché or old clay pots, decorated to look like animals, toys, cars, or any of a wide variety of objects. Traditional piñatas have seven points or cones, that represent the seven capital sins in Catholicism. Candies and other treats are stuffed inside, then the piñata is hung in the air. Children swing a stick or bat at them, often blindfolded, hoping to break the piñata open and release the goodies hidden inside. Symbolically, when kids smash the piñata, they're aiming to destroy sin. Of course, everything is about having fun and no one thinks of that during the festivities. Once the treats are released, watch out as all of the children grab what they can with gusto!

Why does Las Posadas last nine nights? Some say it's because of the nine days it took Mary and Joseph to travel from Nazareth to Bethlehem. Others see the number as the months of pregnancy. Nine days to party and celebrate and contemplate great principles! What could be more fun? Add in community and neighbors and you've got a beautiful recipe for success and connection, something we can all use more of.

Easy Ways To Celebrate

- ★ Eat tamales, or learn how to make them!

- ★ Meditate on the principles, choose one each day as a theme.

- ★ Sing a song or Christmas carol with back and forths.

- ★ Read the story of the nativity.

- ★ Invite your neighbors over for some holiday cheer.

- ★ Add a *piñata* to your holiday décor. Let the children choose the day to break it open!

Multiculturalism are Us

Why do the same old boring December thing? Ruts are so easy to fall into. Mix it up! Consider adding some multiculturalism to your holiday festivities. Find the recipe for chocolate atole and serve it on a cold night. Tell your children the stories of how other cultures celebrate in December. Eat some watermelon or add a pomegranate to your fruit bowl with a prayer for health in the new year. Light a candle and consider the miracle of one day's worth of oil lasting for more than a week.

Take a break from the holiday madness and indulgence to enjoy a simple meal of rice. Embrace compassion and loving kindness. Find an African recipe and consider justice. Teach peace like the Hopi. Make one of your treats a Yule Log, or turn on the fireplace and contemplate Thor. See who in the family remembers what images go with which numbers in the Twelve

Days of Christmas. Turn the tables and let the kids be in charge for an evening or a meal. Read a poem. Take a few moments to reflect on your own inner light, and the many ways you shine.

Take stock of your seed corn and how you plan to manage your resources. December is a great time to re-visualize and regroup. What do you want your next year to look like? Feel like? How can you add more fun and joy?

View yourself as a puzzle. Does everything still fit?

Make prayer sticks or something meaningful as a gift for yourself or another as a different kind of holiday activity.

Take a few moments even in the midst of everything else going on. Breathe. Go ahead. Do it again. Take another breath. Acknowledge all your hard work and progress. Let your body settle. Being frantic never truly serves anyone.

Love yourself a little or a lot. Acknowledge your accomplishments instead of focusing on shortcomings.

Remember that we are all humans on this planet, capable of loving and helping each other, no matter how different our beliefs seem to be. Find a moment to value someone. Smile at a stranger in the grocery store. Compliment a cheerful and effective server. And most of all, appreciate yourself. You are amazing!

Hanukkah

Hanukkah, Hanukkah, festival of lights...
I have a little dreidel no bigger than my thumb...

Many Americans are surprised to learn that Hanukkah is a minor, though well loved, holiday. The major Jewish High Holidays are celebrated in the fall. They are also called the High Holy Days, which cover Rosh Hashanah (the Jewish New Year), Yom Kippur, and the days in between. Other important Jewish holidays include Passover and Purim.

Hanukkah is Hebrew for *dedication*. It is celebrated for eight days in a wintertime Festival of Lights. The timing of Hanukkah is tied to both the lunar and solar calendars. It begins on the 25th of Kislev, three days before the new moon closest to the winter solstice. Kislev is the third month of the civil and the ninth month of the Jewish religious year. Also spelled Ḥanukka, Chanukah, or Chanukkah, it is variously known as the Feast of Dedication, Festival of Lights, or Feast of the Maccabees.

Hanukkah celebrates a miracle. In the second century BCE, the Jewish priestly family known as the Maccabees won a hard-fought victory over the Greeks. The Greeks had outlawed the Jewish religion and taken over their temple to honor Zeus. After the successful rebellion, the Maccabees rededicated the temple at Jerusalem.

The miracle part comes in when they relit the eternal flame on the altar. There was only enough oil to last one day. That one jar of oil miraculously continued to burn for eight days, until more oil could be obtained. This started the candle lighting tradition of the holiday. Let there be light!

Today, the holiday reminds celebrants to rededicate themselves to keeping alive the flame of Jewish religion, culture, and tradition (cue *Fiddler on the Roof*), so that it may be passed on to the next generations. For at least the last thousand years, oily foods have been traditionally eaten on Hanukkah.

Among the most popular dishes are potato *latkes* (pancakes) and *sufganiot* (deep-fried doughnuts).

The celebration of Hanukkah includes a variety of religious and nonreligious customs. The most important of all is the lighting of the *hanukkiah* or *menorah*, a candelabra with eight branches plus a holder for the *shammash* (servant) candle that is used to light the other eight candles. Originally, oil was used as fuel for the menorah. Oil was replaced by candles, which are inserted sequentially each night of the festival. A blessing is offered while the candles are lit.

A traditional Hannukah game is *dreidel*. A dreidel is a spinning top, with four sides, each marked with a different Hebrew letter. The custom of playing dreidel is based on a legend that, during the time of the Maccabees, when Jewish children were forbidden from studying the Torah, they would defy the decree and study anyway. When a Greek official was close by, they would put away their books and take out the spinning tops, claiming they were just playing games.

This Festival of Lights, with candles at the heart of the ritual, makes Hanukkah wonderfully compatible with other traditions. Something about being human makes us all love candles. The steadiness of the flame, while it constantly moves inspires us and reminds us of deeper spiritual truths. The commonality of candles in so many traditions help us understand that we are all seeking the light in our own and varied ways. An excellent reminder for this time of year!

Easy Ways To Celebrate

★ Light a candle (or eight) to honor this tradition.

★ Eat latkes or learn to make them.

★ Contemplate miracles.

★ Spin a top or dreidel.

★ Do a puzzle.

★ Learn what the Hebrew letters on the dreidel are and what they mean.

★ Ask a Jewish friend about their religion and what is important to them in their holiday celebrations.

Let Your Light Shine

Whether lighting candles or celebrating the return of the sun, light is a common theme across December traditions.

What about your own light? Are you feeling shiny and bright? Glowing with hope and faith? Snuffed out? Or just plain lit? Take your own internal temperature. How is your light shining? Is it hiding under a bushel or in the cupboard with the ingredients for cookies? It can be hard with all the busyness of the season to remember that we matter too. Everything starts to fall apart if our mental and emotional health takes second place, or last, or doesn't even make the list at all.

Solutions can be as simple as a cup of tea, or taking a few minutes just to breathe. The restroom can be a refuge for many

of us, especially if there are young children in the household. Treat yourself to a bubble bath or a long hot shower. Check your inner flame. Acknowledge if you need some more fuel, or if the candle is burning at both ends with another flame coming up in the middle. We can't always solve these things instantly. It's still worth checking in within.

Sometimes we need to ask for help. As awkward as it can feel, it's actually doing another person a favor. People love to be of assistance. Perhaps say something like, *"You know what I really would love for Christmas this year? If you could spend an afternoon with the children."* Or *"I need help with my garden way more than anything else."* The gifts of time, energy, and service can be more meaningful and appreciated then any wrapped present.

Often just opening up the topic for conversation can allow unexpected solutions to present themselves that can make everyone happier. *"With not being fully employed, I was stressing about buying gifts this year. I'd love to help you with your project, even if it's brainstorming on the phone or running a few errands for you."*

Creative solutions and being real about what we want and need allows all of our lights to shine just a bit brighter. And they can take some of the stress off and reduce overwhelm to manageable proportions. Shine on!

Saturnalia

Oh my, it's party time! One of the most riotous, hilarious, and topsy-turvy of celebrations, Saturnalia was so beloved by the Romans of the time that they absolutely wouldn't give it up. It ended up morphing into part of what became a Christian celebration when Rome converted.

Saturnalia originated as a winter solstice farmers' festival in Rome. Marking the end of the autumn planting season, it was a feast day for Saturn on December 17th and for Ops, the wife and sister of Saturn, on the 19th. Ops was the Roman goddess of the earth, fertility, wealth, and abundance. Though the original Saturnalia culminated on the 22nd, the celebration was shifted to ending on the 25th. It was a time for feasting, goodwill, generosity to the poor, exchanging gifts, and decorating trees. Here is a truly ancient example of the roots of our modern Christmas trees. Evergreens festooned festivals and halls were decked with greenery. It reminded all that in spite of the presence of winter, spring would come.

Saturnalia saw the reversal of social roles. The wealthy were expected to pay the month's rent for those who couldn't afford it. Masters and slaves swapped clothes. Family households threw dice to determine who would become the temporary Saturnalian monarch.

Older traditions merged in ancient Rome with Saturnalia. Everyone gave themselves up to wild joy. People partied, visited family and friends, and exchanged gifts including sweets and candles. Sound familiar? The holiday ruled, and places were closed, including schools, courts, and businesses.

It was a custom to light candles and roam the streets singing holiday songs, often in the nude! The usual order of the year was suspended. Grudges and quarrels were forgotten. Dress codes were relaxed. Wars were put on hold. A mock king, the *Lord of Misrule*, was crowned. Rich and poor were equal. Slaves were served by masters and children headed the family. Cross-dressing, masquerades, and

merriment of all kinds prevailed. Candles and lamps chased away the spirits of darkness.

From as early as 217 BCE, there were public Saturnalia banquets. In Emperor Domitian's time (51-96 CE), there are records of the lavish banquets and entertainments he presided over, including games which opened with sweets, fruits, and nuts showered on the crowd and featured flights of flamingos released over Rome. Shows with fighting dwarves and female gladiators were illuminated, for the first time, into the night.

Emperor Aurelian (270 to 275 CE) blended a number of pagan solstice celebrations of the nativity of such god-men/saviors as Apollo, Attis, Baal, Dionysus, Helios, Hercules, Horus, Mithra, Osiris, Perscus, and Theseus into a single festival called the *Birthday of the Unconquered Sun* on December 25th.

The conversion of Emperor Constantine to Christianity in 312 CE began the transformation of pagan holidays into Christian ones. Saturnalia continued to be celebrated in the century afterward. It evolved into a popular carnival.

Easy Ways To Celebrate

★ Go to a party or host one.

★ Make a sweet and share it with a neighbor.

★ Drop a grudge.

★ Imagine what you'd do as Lord of Misrule.

★ Sing a holiday song nude (in the shower or your private backyard).

★ Relax your rules.

★ Take a day off.

★ Put the kids in charge for the night.

Yule

We've all heard the words of the famous fa-la-la-la-la Christmas song, *see the blazing yule before us*; yet few of us know the history and roots of this holiday. Many consider Yule to be just another name for Christmas. Its roots are far older and deeper than that. The word *yule* comes from Old Norse and is the name for a twelve-day festival, celebrated by Germanic peoples, from the winter solstice on into January. By the 900s (yes, that long ago), Yule was already merged with the Christian celebration of Christmas.

Yule was associated with the Wild Hunt and the gods Odin and Thor. Thor had a chariot that was pulled across the sky by two goat bucks. During Yule, they would either bring gifts to well-behaved children or demand gifts. Over time, the yule goat has become a symbol of Christmas in Scandinavian countries and is said to carry Father Christmas on his back. Things morphed again and a combination Yule Goat/Santa Claus/Father Christmas would bring gifts and drive a sleigh pulled by reindeer, not goats.

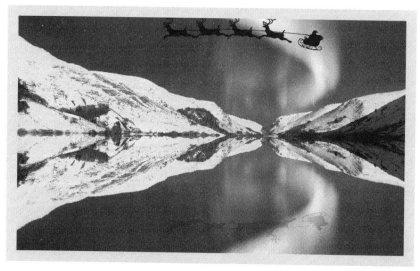

The yule log is a large tree limb or trunk. Trees have been part of these human holiday celebrations for a very long time. So have evergreen decorations. Even in the heart of winter, we know that spring will come. Ancients believed that the longer the yule log burned, the faster the sun would return to warm the earth and bring good luck to the family.

Since the 1800s, the yule log has made an appearance as a cake, shaped like a log called the *Bûche de Noël*, with chocolate frosting bark and candy holly leaves. (Yum!) While no one is positive exactly how the yule log turned into a cake, everyone can agree that it's delicious.

Gingerbread is another sweet associated with Yule. In medieval times, ginger was not commonly available until the Crusaders brought it back in the eleventh century. There were even laws affecting its use, since it was rare. Gingerbread was only allowed to be produced during the holidays, so it became another special and unusual treat associated with winter and Yule.

Then and now, Yule is aligned with gatherings that include merriment, feasting, fire, and gifts. The ancient traditions continue. The exact timing on Yule changes a bit from year to year. It starts around the solstice goes and through the first of the new year. Perfect timing for joyous and nature-filled festivities!

Easy Ways To Celebrate

★ Explore Scandinavian and Germanic traditions

★ Read a book or watch a movie about Odin or Thor, even a comic book!

★ Enjoy a fire.

★ Make or buy a candied yule log.

★ Sing fa-la-la-la-la at the top of your lungs.

★ Eat gingerbread (oh darn!).

★ Have a cup of ginger tea.

★ Decorate with greenery.

Self-Care

How do we take care of ourselves this December? With the holidays upon us and the ever-present concerns of the outer world, even a moment of calm may seem like too much to hope for. How do we plan? With so much to do and think about, it would frazzle a saint! How do we manage with some modicum of grace, comfort, and ease?

Start small. Grab moments when you can. Remember to breathe. Such simple advice, but so potent when practiced. Remind yourself that all of this busyness is in service to something. It's often about letting the people we love know we love them. Get rooted in that. Consider gifting presence rather than presents. Often, just someone to share the overwhelm with can make a huge difference.

Cut yourself some slack. Look at that do-list and be cutthroat about eliminating things. Schedule some time for yourself to just

be alone. Put it on your calendar and don't give it up no matter how tempting or urgent the request for your time sounds. *"Sorry, I've got an appointment at 3:00 that I just can't move."* No one needs to know that appointment is with yourself.

Think about what floats your boat and make sure you have access to that, whether it's a walk in nature or the park, a favorite puzzle, or your fuzzy blanket. And when you get those stolen moments, relish them!

Nothing is more important than your sanity at this time. Do what it takes to keep yourself on as even a keel as possible. If you have trouble with stress management, have a list handy of things that help. And when the going gets tough, ask a friend to be your stress buddy. Have someone you can call and vent to when it all becomes too much. No one available? Do it yourself! Write, draw, or record what you would say if you could talk to a friend. And then, be there for yourself. Sounds a little wacky, but it works.

When quiet comes, sink into it. Embrace it. Delight in it.

Hang in there. The holidays will soon pass. Decide how to create some glowing memory treasures and then make it happen. You have the power!

And do remember to breathe. Connect with loved ones. Connect with yourself. Give yourself permission to take care of you right along with everyone else.

Revel in moments of friendship, joy, and grace. Those are the parts you'll remember, not all the frantic stuff. Light a candle. Stoke your own inner flame. Create a loving connection with someone who means a lot to you. That's the most priceless treasure, and a present that will last a lifetime.

Christian Christmas Traditions

Advent

Advent means *coming* in Latin. This observance is of the coming of Jesus into the world. Christians use the four Sundays and weeks of Advent to prepare and remember the real meaning of Christmas. No one is really sure when Advent was first celebrated but it dates back to at least 567.

In 567, the Council of Tours proclaimed the twelve days from Christmas to Epiphany on January 6th as a sacred and festive season. Advent fasting was recommended in preparation for the feast.

Advent begins on the

Sunday that falls between November 27th and December 3rd each year. There are several ways that Advent is counted down but the most common is by a calendar or candles. Many of us have seen the calendars where you open up a window each day; some of them even include small treats or toys.

There are three meanings of *coming* that grace Advent. The first happened about two thousand years ago when Jesus came into the world as a baby to live as a man. The second *coming* describes Jesus returning to earth as a holy being in the future. The third is a very personal, *coming* of Jesus as the Prince of Peace, bringing love, kindness, and compassion into the hearts of believers.

To balance the two elements of remembrance and anticipation, the first two Sundays in Advent look forward to his second coming, and the last two Sundays look backward to remember the birth. The four weeks are broken down into themes:

1. Hope (or promise)

2. Preparation (waiting or prophecy)

3. Joy (peace)

4. Love (adoration)

Advent wreaths have four candles. Created out of evergreens, they symbolize everlasting life in the midst of winter and death. Additional decorations, like holly and berries, are sometimes added. Families light candles each Sunday.

As a religious celebration, Advent is meant to be a season of fasting. Fasting can take forms other than not eating. Some choose to take a break from the internet. Some stop going to movies, or avoid all violence. Some volunteer. The intent is to clear the mind and heart to prepare for the deep celebration to come.

Contemplate the Miracle that is You

However you do December, consider personalizing your holidays this year. Bring in some other cultures and traditions. Widen your world. Experiment. Have some fun! Find what resonates with you and your family and friends. Be inclusive. Take pieces and moments from various traditions and adapt them into your own. Or take a deeper dive into the mysteries that exist in your belief system or religion. There's always room for wonder and joy. And we can all use a little bit, or a lot, of fun.

Exercise your creativity and let the ideas and silliness flow. It can be a stressful time of year. Leaven the stress with fun and joy and puzzles and play and fellowship and love. Embrace the coming light in whatever form it takes in your world. Be kind and gentle with yourself and others. Let some things fall off the to-do list and don't worry about it. Give yourself the gift of grace.

Take care of yourself. Your health and state of mind matter. Say no if you feel uncomfortable, or just plain don't want to do something. Let some things go. It's okay. Limit your gift exchanges. We're often surprised to discover that people are relieved rather than disappointed.

Let your beautifully unique light shine. Celebrate in ways that feel good to you and yours. Tis the season of miracles. Remember that you are one. Treasure yourself accordingly.

Christmas

The long-awaited day finally arrives. The children almost can't believe that it is finally, finally, finally here. They've been looking forward to this forever! The deeply religious have an amazing opportunity to profoundly renew

their faith. Songs that have become annoying take on new, and deeper meaning.

Christmas is on December 25th. For two millennia, people have been observing it with traditions and practices that are both religious and secular. Not only is it a sacred religious holiday, it's a worldwide cultural and commercial phenomenon

Like Saturnalia, Christmas apparently started in Rome. It then spread to the eastern Mediterranean, making its way to Scandinavia by the eighth century. Easter was by far and away the most important holiday for early Christians. The birthday of Jesus of Nazareth was not observed. It was in the fourth century that the church came up with the concept of celebrating Jesus' birth as a special holiday.

December 25th became the chosen day. Winter Solstice and early winter festivals harmonized the return of the Sun and the birth of the Son. By blending them, church leaders increased the chances that Christmas would be popularly embraced. By the Middle Ages, Christianity was the main religion in the western world.

Like today's sacred celebrations, believers attended church for Christmas. What happened after church in the Middle Ages, however, was often closer to Mardi Gras than a calmly devout religious celebration. The crowning of a Lord of Misrule was a part of the party. Christmas got so wild and crazy in the American colonies, that from 1659 to 1681, it was actually outlawed in Boston, and law-breakers were fined five shillings.

It wasn't until later in the nineteenth century that Americans re-invented Christmas, and changed it from a raucous carnival holiday into a family-centered day of peace and nostalgia. In the early 1800s, Christmas was a time of protest and social unrest. What changed?

Two literary books were hugely impactful, and we can't underestimate the influence of the Queen of England on American Christmas celebrations. The books were *A Christmas Carol* by Charles Dickens and a series of stories by Washington Irving, published in 1819 (the Washington Irving of *The Legend of Sleepy Hollow* and *Rip Van Winkle* fame). The stories described a made-up Christmas celebration in an English manor that embraced an idealism that America was craving at the time. People getting along together regardless of class or station or economic status and enjoying "traditions"; some of which Irving made up out of thin air! He invented what we now consider to be true traditions of the season. Clearly it resonated, because people embraced it whole heartedly, and still do.

Around the same time, English author Charles Dickens created the classic holiday tale, *A Christmas Carol*. The story's message of the importance of charity and goodwill towards all humankind struck a powerful chord in the United States and England. God bless us everyone!

As Christmas became the ideal family holiday for Americans, the next hundred years saw it evolve. Old customs were unearthed. People looked toward recent immigrants and churches to see how the day ought to be celebrated.

Americans honor their melting pot heritage around Christmas, pulling ideas and decorations and concepts from all over the world and blending them. We exchange

Christmas cards and gifts, definitely crossing class and economic lines. We have German glass ornaments on our homegrown trees, Italian candy, ginger, and other treats that harken back to Yule, and so much more! Take a look around your house and at your tree, if you have one, and consider all of the myriad traditions and cultures represented. Melting pot indeed! And speaking of Christmas trees...

O Christmas Tree

Americans didn't really embrace the tree custom until a drawing of Queen Victoria's decorated Christmas tree was on the cover of the *Illustrated London News* in the 1840s. The rest, as they say, is history. Prince Albert was from Germany and fondly remembered trees decorated with candles and ornaments from his youth. Fashionable society on the east coast loved emulating the royals, and Christmas trees became a thing. A huge thing!

Christmas trees are grown in every state in America, including Alaska and Hawaii. They've been sold commercially in the United States since around 1850. More than a million acres of land are used to grow trees. 1912 marked the first community Christmas tree in New York City. At last count, there are over one hundred million Christmas trees displayed worldwide. The first tree in Rockefeller Center in New York City was placed in 1931. It was unadorned, with no ornaments, and put there by construction workers. Two years later, another arrived. Lights were added and the decorating began. The tallest, a Norway spruce, arrived in 1948 and was one hundred feet tall! Today the Rockefeller Center tree has over 25,000 lights.

The first record of Christmas trees in America was in Pennsylvania in the 1830s, brought by German settlers. The roots go back much longer and deeper than that. The early Egyptians decorated their palm trees for their twelve-day

festival in ancient times. The Vikings believed evergreens to be sacred to their sun god. Yule, Saturnalia, and Solstice celebrations include decorated trees and/or greenery. The reminder that spring really will come again is important when you're cold and knee-deep in winter. Brrrr!

According to folklore, Martin Luther (1483-1546) is credited with creating the first formal Christmas tree including lights (candles). The story goes that he was walking home through the woods and contemplating the Christmas miracle, when he looked up and saw the stars shining through the branches of the trees. He wanted to share the image with his wife and family. Voilà!

Chances are good that trees were already being brought home and decorated, but Martin Luther is supposedly the one that added candles. It makes such a great story! Regardless of who started it, by the sixteenth and seventeenth centuries, Christmas trees with candles were a well-established tradition in Germany. Hence Prince Albert. As German immigrants spanned the globe, their Christmas trees with candles and other decorations went with them. Edward Johnson, one of Thomas Edison's associates, created electrical Christmas tree lights in 1882. A much safer choice.

Back to Christmas

Americans today continue to celebrate Christmas by exchanging gifts, attending church, sharing meals and treats with family and friends, and, of course, waiting for Santa Claus to arrive. Practicing Christians light candles in church on Christmas Eve and contemplate the brotherhood of man and a miraculous birth. Merry Christmas to all, and to all a good night!

Easy Ways To Celebrate

- ★ Decorate a tree or a plant.

- ★ Make a gift.

- ★ Share a gift.

- ★ Offer a treat to a friend or neighbor.

- ★ Bake cookies and share them around.

- ★ Light candles.

- ★ Sing carols, even go caroling!

- ★ Take a quiet moment and reflect on the miracles in your beliefs.

- ★ Contemplate peace on earth and goodwill to all.

The Twelve Days of
Christmas (Twelvetide)

The thing many of us are most familiar with about the Twelve Days of Christmas is the song. The easiest parts to remember are the five gold rings and the partridge, but the rest can get pretty confusing, especially when we get to lords-a-leaping, ladies dancing, and pipers piping. And is it seven swans and six geese or the other way around? How

many maids are milking and who is dancing? Here is the order to clear up any confusion.

One the first day of Christmas
My true love gave to me...

A Partridge in a Pear Tree
Two Turtle Doves,
Three French Hens,
Four Calling/Collie Birds,
Five Golden Rings,
Six Geese-a-Laying,
Seven Swans-a-Swimming,
Eight Maids-a-Milking,
Nine Ladies Dancing,
Ten Lords-a-Leaping,
Eleven Pipers Piping,
Twelve Drummers Drumming

The history of the carol is a bit confusing. It first appeared in the late eighteenth century in a book called *Mirth Without Mischief*. Many think the melody sounds French. The song was updated by English composer Frederic Austin in 1909. The original song was designed as a memory game. If you forgot the words, you had to pay a forfeit, often a kiss! Sometimes favors were offered or exchanged.

Favors can get expensive. In the fun fact department, PNC is one of the largest banks in the United States. They create a Christmas Price Index and calculated the cost if you were to buy all the gifts in the song. The total estimate in 2019 came to a whopping $38,993.59. That's a 95% increase from the first Christmas Price Index in 1984.

In England in the Middle Ages, Twelvetide was a period of continuous feasting and merrymaking, which climaxed on Twelfth Night, the traditional end of the Christmas season. Often a Lord of Misrule was chosen to lead the revels. Later, William Shakespeare used it as the setting for one of his most famous plays, *Twelfth Night*.

Many Americans are surprised to discover that the first day of Christmas is actually on Christmas Day itself. All those Advent Calendars and the keen anticipation with which children look forward to Christmas leave us thinking that the twelve days must start earlier.

As a religious holiday, Twelvetide honors the nativity of Jesus. The timing marks the span between his birth and

the arrival of the Magi, the three wise men. It begins on December 25th and runs through January 5th, followed by Epiphany on January 6th, sometimes called Three Kings' Day.

Christians who observe the twelve days may give gifts on each of them, with each of the days representing a wish for a corresponding month of the new year. Many feast and otherwise celebrate the entire time through the morning of the solemnity of Epiphany.

Modern practices include lighting a candle for each day, singing the verse of the corresponding day from the famous song, and lighting a yule log on Christmas Eve, letting it burn a bit on each of the twelve nights. For some, the Twelfth Night remains the night of the most festive parties and gift exchanges. Some households exchange gifts on the first and last days. As in former times, the Twelfth Night to the morning of Epiphany is the time during which Christmas trees and decorations are taken down and put away.

Service

One of the great Christian values practiced in December is that of service. Whether it is volunteering to serve a holiday meal to those in need or contributing to a deserving cause, this time of year encourages people to reflect on what is important. What does it mean to be human, and how can we help?

Most spiritual and religious traditions place a high value on the power of prayer. Spare a thought or a prayer or an energy beam for those who need help, whether with health or money or a personal crisis. This time of year can be hard on people. Send out some good vibes. Remember to put yourself on the good vibe list.

What helps you get through? For many it is art, music, spiritual practices, community, and food. Preparing it, consuming it,

sharing it, enjoying it, food makes great people glue. Friendship and connection help too. Having someone to vent with on bad days is critical. Knowing that others understand what we are going through helps us to not feel so alone and isolated. The folks who step forward to make things better for everyone are amazing. Let them know you notice and value and appreciate them.

If someone has helped you get through and improved the quality of your life, tell them. Say thank you. Send a card or flowers. Tip those musicians who saved your sanity. Thank those grocery store clerks and other service people who improve the quality of your life.

Service is deeply embedded in our December history. It's amazing how helping others helps us feel good, not just about ourselves, but about everyone. No one has to know if you prefer to keep your service private. It's a sacred thing. Try it and see how you feel. Every iota of energy sent will be received. Let someone know they helped you. Smile.

Peace on Earth. Goodwill to all.

We've all become heroes in our own mythic stories. Consider your cape and give it a fluff. The super power of getting through December gracefully and joyously is yours!

Kwanzaa

Kwanzaa is an African-American festival of life from December 26th to January 1st. It is a celebration of unity and a way to acknowledge those who have gone before. Seven days of fun and music, food and family, dancing and creativity; what could be more delightful? And there's deep principles underneath it all. Kwanzaa is similar to Thanksgiving in the United States and the Yam Festival in Ghana and Nigeria. The word *kwanzaa* means *first* in Swahili.

Founded in 1966 by Dr. Maulana Karenga, Kwanzaa (also spelled Kwanza) is a ritual to welcome the first harvests to the home. It is also a way to recognize African-American heritage. Ideals around community, justice, family, and nature are celebrated and explored. Dr. Karenga created this festival as a response to the commercialism of Christmas. Though it celebrates African roots and values, it is not a traditional holiday in Africa; it is all American.

Five common sets of values are central to the activities of the week: *ingathering, reverence, commemoration, recommitment,* and *celebration*. Each of the seven days focuses on a different concept. They are collectively known as *Nguzo Saba*:

Umoja or unity
Kujichagulia or self-determination
Ujima or collective work and responsibility
Ujamaa or cooperative economics
Nia or purpose
Kuumba or creativity
Imani or faith

Like Hanukkah, candles are central to Kwanzaa. The candelabra is called the *kinara*. It holds three red, three green, and one black candle. The candles are lit in order until the final day when all seven candles are burned at once. Ears of corn are placed under the kinara, one for each child in the family, to celebrate the harvest and hope for the future.

A feast known as *karamu* is held on December 31st. African dishes are often part of the menu. This is the day that honors creativity (kuumba), so it's a great day for crafts. Participants greet one another with *Habari gani* which is Swahili for *How are you/How's the news with you?*

Gifts are exchanged on January 1st and frequently handmade treasures are some of them. Kwanzaa helps bring the past year into focus, and encourages deep thought about community and the future. What a fulfilling way to review the old and think about the new!

Easy Ways To Celebrate

★ Have a Kwanzaa feast or add an African dish to your December menu.

★ Make crafts part of your festivities.

★ Celebrate what you have harvested this year.

★ Contemplate hope for the future.

★ Light a candle and meditate on the *Nguzo Saba* and how they might apply to your community, as well as your personal goals.

Endgame: The Most Wonderful Time of the Year

Our dozen December delights have brought us so much to celebrate and so many festivals and cultures to learn from and enjoy. Time traveling through the northern hemisphere's traditions has been a stroll through the history of human community.

Celebrations come in many shapes, sizes, colors, forms, and flavors. We've expanded our concepts of what and how to celebrate. Some of the same old traditions and gatherings just don't seem to fit anymore.

Here's a patchwork word quilt taken from the traditions to remind us of our unity through diversity. Collected here together, they read as a poetic message for us all. It's a cornucopia of delight!

Habari gani? How's the news with you?

Feel the light of the moon and stars upon your face as the

time of darkness lingers and grows. Feel the earth beneath your feet.

Light candles and be a light. Nurture your own inner flame. Your beautiful unique light blesses all.

There is always room for wonder and joy.

Remember that many traditions share the belief and imagery of the eternal flame. It lights our hearts. It nourishes our souls. It is there for everyone. It is not possible to extinguish, though many have tried.

Pondering our options is customary for this time of year. We turn inward and reflective and reach out to others to share our collective love.

The most important present is presence. Whatever and however you celebrate, have a warm, safe, cozy, comfortable, and delightful holiday season. Let your loved ones know they are loved and cared for. No matter how our connections happen, they are heartfelt.

If someone has helped you get through and improved the quality of your life, tell them. Say thank you.

Be kind and gentle with yourself and others.

Give yourself permission to take care of yourself right along with everyone else.

Notice the rebirth of the sun. Celebrate the return of the light. Tame the monsters of chaos. Drop a grudge. Acknowledge your accomplishments. Plan for the coming year. Bless your home. Teach peace.

Exercise your creativity and let your ideas and silliness flow.

From dumplings to tsampa to tamales to latkes to corn to watermelon to peanut soup to rice to tang yuan to gingerbread, eat, drink, and be merry. Dance and sing. Share the love.

Reach out to neighbors with some holiday cheer. Eat an orange. Read and/or write a poem. Remember to have fun and check in with your inner self.

Celebrate miracles in all forms: oil that lasts for eight days, virgin birth, enlightenment under a fig tree, flying goats and reindeer, and fat guys who fit down a chimney.

Count your blessings. Meditate on all you are grateful for. Say a little prayer for yourself and your life. Right here. Right now.

Play! Spin a dreidel or bat a piñata or elect a Lord of Misrule. Be a Lord of Misrule for a day or an evening and see what fun you can have!

View yourself as a puzzle and see if your pieces fit together differently now.

Celebrate our unity through our December diversity. Contemplate marvels, principles, and what really matters the most. Happy Hopi-days!

Embrace the coming year in whatever form it takes for you. The world needs all of us.

Love yourself a little or a lot.

Revel in moments of friendship, joy, and grace.

Bring love, kindness, and compassion into your heart.

Tis the season of miracles. Remember that you are one. Treasure yourself accordingly.

Smile.

You are the light.

Peace on Earth.
Goodwill to all.

Gratitude and Appreciation

Thanks so much to our community of amazing folks who supported the making of this book—Bertha Edington, Darity Wesley, Ingrid Coffin, and Paula Wansley. Elaine Chan, Isabel Oliver, Jerry Flack, Jim Giles, and Lisa Tansey provided input on specific holiday details. Valerie Costa was our awesome editor. The cover and interior design by Christy Day of Constellation Book Services.

Melissa Morgan contributed her wisdom, extraordinary expertise and talent to this book. Here's her bio:

Melissa Morgan is a harpist, composer, teacher, and recording artist. She is also a writer and editor. Collaborating with Cristina Smith, she is the editor for the whole award-winning Yoga for the Brain series, as well as other books.

When she's not on tour, Melissa lives, writes, edits, teaches, works, and plays in San Diego, California.

The images were created by many talented artists globally and licensed on Dreamstime.com. Model releases included in Dreamstime license.

Cristina Smith

The December Dozen: A Celebration of Holidays is award-winning author Cristina Smith's 12th book. She has been writing about the interesting origins of holidays since before the turn of century in newspaper articles, blogs and newsletters. Cristina and her brother Rick are the co-authors of nine puzzle books together: six in the award-winning, best-selling *Yoga for the Brain* series and three others from Rockridge Press, two sudoku and one word search.

Cristina was a chef as a part of her entrepreneurial career, which led to her collaborating with celebrity chef Ron Oliver on *The Great Gatsby Cookbook: Five Fabulous Roaring '20s Parties* with Post Hill Press.

An avid reader, writer, book coach, community builder, and celebrator of the richness of life, Cristina lives tucked away in the fabulous forest community of Nevada City, CA.

Other books by Cristina Smith include:

Life Wisdom Word Search: Yoga for the Brain *with Rick Smith and 60 Contributing Authors*

Inspired Wisdom Word Search: Yoga for the Brain *with Rick Smith and 60 Contributing Authors*

Animal Wisdom Word Search: Yoga for the Brain *with Rick Smith and Lauren McCall*

The Word Search Sage: Yoga for the Brain *with Rick Smith and Ingrid Coffin*

The Word Search Oracle: Yoga for the Brain *with Rick Smith and Darity Wesley*

The Tao of Sudoku: Yoga for the Brain *with Rick Smith*

Contact Cristina at
www.YogaForTheBrain.com

Get your free Yoga for the Brain
companion puzzle for this book at
www.DecemberDozen.com

Made in the USA
Las Vegas, NV
14 December 2024

14242982R00061